Aliens, Fallen Angels, Nephilim and the Supernatural

What Ancient Bible Secrets and Prophecies reveal about these Supernatural Forces

by Robert Rite

Table of Contents

Get Complimentary Access to: "Prophecy Alerts"

Dear Reader: Prophecies are being fulfilled so rapidly in these last days that I am offering my readers complimentary access to "*prophecy alerts*" so that you get "*Breaking Prophecy News*" as soon as it breaks...Just follow this link below and sign Up today...
http://robertritebooks.com/prophecy-alerts/

Introduction

Does the Bible reveal the inter-relationship between Aliens, Fallen Angels, Demons and the Nephilim? Yes it does! The bible says much about the supernatural. In this book we will dive into the hidden truth about these supernatural forces.

After having been deceived as kids about Santa Clause, the tooth fairy, and other myths, most of us refuse to believe or accept anything that we cannot see, hear or touch. We have all been taught to be a "doubting Thomas".

Skepticism is always healthy, but when it comes to the supernatural if the bible clearly reveals that supernatural forces are all around us - then we can and should take it seriously.

I am prepping you, because I will be covering the supernatural realm in this book. Much of what you will read here may seem as bizarre as to rival the most bizarre Science fiction movie.

But I must prepare you for things that are coming upon the earth in the near future that will make many men's hearts fail because it will be just that hard to take in! So let's get started!

Chapter 1 - What God Reveals

God reveals many supernatural mysteries within the bible.

Indeed, the bible is the "ultimate guidebook to the supernatural". Jesus warned us that the end will be just like it was in the days of Noah **(Luke 17:26)**.

We learn in Genesis that in the beginning God intended for every life form to re-produce in its own kind (**Genesis 1 verses 11, 12, 24-25**). And in **Genesis 1:26** God reveals that he made us in his own image.

God intended for man to rule the entire earth in total peace, and harmony. In the Garden of Eden there was to be no illness and no death and man was not intended to die. It was to be Heaven on earth!

In fact Adam and Eve had they not sinned, may have allowed all of us to enjoy eternal life here on earth since the TREE of LIFE was also in the midst of the Garden of Eden, and had God allowed them to eat the fruit of that tree, they (and we) would have lived forever! We read in Genesis 2:9 that the Tree of life was in the midst of the Garden of Eden. In Genesis 2:16-17 we learn that they could eat of any tree (including the Tree of Life) except for the tree of the knowledge of good and evil. And in Genesis 3:22-24, God reveals that He had to expel Adam and Eve from the Garden so that they may not eat of the tree of life (because of their sin). *Folks, this is how close we came to*

And as we all know, Adam and Eve disobeyed the Word of God and listened to the voice of Lucifer. They put Man's reason and logic above the Word of God. The result was the fall of man. War, chaos, sin disease, weather changes, decay and death entered the world. In addition, Lucifer gained the temporary legal right to be the ruler of this world.

In the end of chapter 3 we learn that God expelled them from the garden and restricted access to the tree of Life that would have given them eternal life (**Genesis 3:24**)

God then reveals in **Genesis chapter 6:1-4** how Satan immediately attacked God's perfect plan to create man in his own image, by having fallen angels mate with women creating unholy mutants (called the Nephilim) attempting to corrupt the DNA of man!

Because of this unholy abomination, God had to destroy the whole earth with a great flood in order to destroy the Nephilim seed and fallen man who had willingly corrupted the DNA of almost all mankind, save Noah and his immediate family. I cover more on the Nephilim in the next chapter and how they most likely are the ancestors of any "Aliens" that might be out there. But first, it is important here to note that these creatures were descendents of the fallen angels, and so upon their death, their spirits would remain alive on earth and would take on the role of demons.

Chapter 2 - So who are the Nephilim?

As noted, the Nephilim are the result of fallen angels mating with women and thus polluting the gene pool. Prior to this abomination, man's DNA was perfect. That is why we read in the ancient scriptures how men lived upwards of 900 years or longer with almost no disease before the flood (Genesis 5:5). Then after the flood man's lifespan was reduced to 120 years. Later on Man's lifespan would decrease further to around 70 years or so.

Nephilim is derived from the word Nephal; the offspring of the fallen angels are referred to as: a bully or tyrant, inferior to man, corrupted, one who falls (less than what God created us to be) See **Genesis 2:21, Numbers 5:21, Numbers 6:12**

This Nephilim may be the ancient race that developed highly advanced technology and built the massive antediluvian structures such as the Stonehenge, the Egyptian pyramids, and Incan and Mayan temples, all of which incorporated human sacrifice in ancient occult religions. Also, the nations that occupied the land of Israel (the Hittites, Jebusites, Amorites, Hivites, etc.) that God had the Israelites fully destroy (man, wife and children) was perhaps because they were descendants of the Nephilim!

Before the Flood of Noah a secret hybrid race of fallen angels breeding with human women was designed by Satan to circumvent God's plans and create a race of satanic supermen who would rule the world (sort of like satanic inspired Hitler, wanted Nazi Germany to morph into). And this breeding of this race of god-men or supermen is an essential Satan inspired theme of all occult-based religions throughout history. Adolph Hitler hoped to use this Science of Eugenics to scientifically breed a new master race of supermen or god-men.

Nephilim like mutations were also produced through the mixing of human DNA with animals. As if the Nephilim were not enough, Satan had the fallen angels teach men how to experiment with and mix the DNA of humans with animals so as to create creatures that were part human and part animal! This explains why in ancient hieroglyphics and writings we see images depicting many beings that were part human and part animal.

We also read and see this in Greek, Roman, and Egyptian literature and culture; not to mention Mythological figures such as Zeus, Apollo, Hercules and many others (The later possibly being Nephilim). We also read of ancient writings on rocks that reveal some of the teachings of the fallen angels (called Watchers).

Arphaxad's son of Kainam (who was a relative of Noah) (read Jubilees 8:1-5), discovered a rock that documents teachings of the watchers – and he did what they taught.

In all ancient cultures - Greek, Roman, Egyptian we find chimera's like Sadders which are part human mixed with animals! **Ezekiel 1:5-10** (talks about a sadder – which is part man but has wings – but created by God – so maybe the fallen angels want to create in their image by creating human-animal hybrids – in their image).

All these Greek "god(s)"; stories of renown may be the worship of the Nephilim (Idol, demon, and Satan Worship). This is just as Satan would have wanted to happen, and this practice of idol worship sadly goes on today!

But you and I know better. We know that we are created in God's image – whereas Nephilim, demons, aliens, and all these so called "gods" are all created in the image of Satan, and thus are inherently evil by nature.

Researchers in the field believe that these Nephilim originally grew to over 36 feet tall and gradually in time would grow smaller to around 10 feet or so. This adds credence to the story of Goliath during David's time (1 Samuel 17:49).

Genesis 6:4 (This is all Pre-Flood) reveals the following: "there were giants in the earth in those days; and also after that." Giants being the Nephilim. The whole earth had become corrupt, not just the Nephilim and the fallen angels. The reason being, as the book of Jasher 4:18 (which will be discussed in a later chapter) teaches us is that humans - referred to as the sons of men in the bible (and not just the sons of God - who are the fallen angels) started to manipulate and mixing the gene pool and animals with men. The days of Jared were marked with the creation of angel-human hybrids, whereas the days of

Noah were marked with creation of animal-human hybrids.

These Nephilim giants also lived during Moses and Abraham's time. They seemed to have returned after the flood perhaps cause of Lots son's wives who were chosen by Noah just before the flood and may have had some Nephilim DNA.

The bible indicates that those NOT written in the book of life are the Nephilim, fallen angels, and of course as Revelation reveals, any human being who take the mark of the beast (**Revelation 14:9-10**)

Nephilim existed within the Canaanites, Hittites, Jebusites and other societies that occupied land that God would later have the Israelites conquer. This would explain why God instructed the Israelites to destroy entire civilizations (including the men, wives, children and their animals). This was to secure our salvation, by purifying his Land us from the corrupted DNA.

The good news is that Gods mighty men were able to fight and win against the Giborim (Nephillim) just like when David beat Goliath. Below are several versus that may refer to the Nephilim

How did Nephilim (Giants) survive the flood?

So how did some of these Nephilim survive the flood since we learn that the Israelites had to fight off these giants who occupied the Promised Land? After all Noah and his wife were pure. Well scripture says that Noah was pure, his wife was from Enoch (a God fearing man) so she was pure. Their 3 sons were also pure. But what about the son's wives? Noah chose the son's wives just seven days before the great flood so that it was possible that they were not pure. **Genesis 6:18** after **Genesis 6:12** (Note here that God said all were corrupt).

Why would God allow Nephilim to survive the flood?

God may have allowed this for his Glory through Israel's fighting forces. The Israelites had to fight off these giants who occupied the Promised Land. The tribes that God commanded the Israelites to totally destroy (including the wives, children and animals) had Nephilim DNA. These tribes included the "ites; including the Canaanites, Hittites, Amorites, Perizzites, Jebusites, and Hivites.

Bible References to the Nephilim:

- **Canaan** Genesis 10:15-19 these are the *"ites"* that the children of Israel constantly had to kill.

- **Mizraim:** He begat Caphtor (Genesis 10:13,14) settled in Crete and was the father of the philistines (Jeremiah 47:4, Amos 9:7), these were giants. All of the Greek Mythology characters originated in Crete. (Goliath and his brothers also came from here)

- **Cush**: Married Semiramis and begat Nimrod (means = we shall rebel).

- **Nimrod** "began to be a mighty one in the earth..." this perhaps means that either he became a powerful man naturally, or became a giant or great hunter of giants through genetic alterations. **Genesis 10:8,9**

- **Baalbek** – Is just one of several large fortresses - was built 5000 years back – during the time of the tower of Babel. This fortress must have been built by Giants, die to huge rock structures weighing several tons each. They were constructed of columns that were so massive that not even heavy equipment of today can move them.

- **Genesis 14 war**: There was also a battle of 9 Giants written of in **Genesis 14:5-9**. Some of these were Rephaims, Zuzims in Ham, Emins, Horites, Amalekites, Amorites. These were all grandchildren of Noah. **Genesis 14:10**

- Numbers 13:33 Refers to the sons of Anak (descendant of Canaan) as being giants. Note that it took 2 men to carry a cluster of grapes on a pole – these were genetically manufactured grapes made to feed the Nephilim (giants).

- **Exodus 20:4,5, Numbers 14:18** – God warned that he would visit the iniquity to 4th generation of those who hate God (anyone who worships Satan or who rejects God and his commandments).

NOTE: People who committed adultery or other sins tend to have a genetic marker (a scar) in a certain place in their DNA, that is passed on to their offspring. But these scars are reversible through repentance and loving the Lord (becoming a God fearing Christian).

- **Ham's line** may have had Nephilim

- **The Curses and blessings upon the children**: Deuteronomy 7:9 (loving God),

- **Joshua 11:22** – very few Nephilim remained in the land of the children of Israel after Israel fought them off – they only remained in Gaza, Gath, Ashdod – and how ironic that these remain geopolitical hotspots whose inhabitants still torment the Israelites.

Chapter 3 - Aliens, UFOs and the Nephilim Connection

I used to believe that Aliens were just a big lie (Like the tooth fairy). But now I believe
that they may exist - but with a HUGE caveat.

If they exist, then aliens must be demonic creatures. Let's use just a bit of common sense here - if God created man in his own image (obviously a superior being above ALL other beings), then why have many fallen to Satan's deception that there exists beings that are superior to us out there? It just defies all common sense, wouldn't you agree?

Important Note: Satan wants us to believe that we are weak imperfect mortals, and that we are not the most intelligent physical beings out there. That there exists a far superior race of intelligent physical beings in the form of aliens, out there, somewhere. Well sorry all you science fiction lovers, but that is all really what it is - science fiction! It is totally contrary to what the Bible teaches us.

God said "let us make man in OUR image, according to our LIKENESS" **Genesis 1:26. Since we were created in God's likeness and image - it is obviously highly unlikely that there exists a more perfect and intelligent creation out there than mankind, which was made in God's very own image!**

Fallen angels may be misidentified as aliens. Aliens are just another satanic deception into making us feel inferior to some supposed "superior" intelligent life (even though God made man in HIS OWN image!!!). Do Not be deceived; remember that there are no entities or intelligent creatures except those spoken of clearly in the Bible. Keep in mind that angels can take the form of a man (and other creature like forms for that matter). Because of his supernatural powers, it is easy for the Devil to trick many (unfamiliar with the word of God) into believing in Aliens and extraterrestrial life.

Demons are the disembodied spirits of the Nephilim - so to live on they have to occupy a human body or a biological suit (like grey suits; ET). It's all about the joining of 2 species; in this case a demonic mutation.

Aliens are creations of fallen angels just like the Nephilim. For those who report alien abductions, perhaps these "aliens" may be conducting genetic experiments to bring about a last days incursion with demonically enhanced human beings. Demons do occupy the flesh of humans (demonic possessions - also referenced throughout the bible) so this may all be a part of Satan's grand plan.

I believe that if Aliens do indeed exist, and do indeed abduct humans, they are controlled by Satan and their purpose is to alter the human DNA (just like in ancient times). We do not just hear about human abductions, we also hear and read reports about cattle that seem to have been left dead in many fields void of blood and their internal organs. Whether by Devil worshippers, Chupacabra, or aliens, they all have the same footprint.

Throughout the world we see cattle (sheep, cows) mutilations - being deprived of their brains, organs, and all their blood like a sacrificial ritual (Chupacabra may be a real alien demon). They leave no trace - i.e. tire tracks, blood on ground - giving a Supernatural footprint, or should I say lack thereof! They prefer cattle and sheep just like the ancient rituals - which of course are demonic controlled.

They want to mix God's DNA in man since they cannot create all they can do is mess with God's DNA and mix it to create a body that they can control in accord to their own wish desire, in their full control. But God prevents this mixing because God knew that this would ultimately create bad - evil genetics - the fruit of which would be evil mutations - perhaps superior in certain characteristics just like angels and fallen angels - but corrupted and thus subject to eternal damnation - not eternal life which is Satan's desire and his deception.

Some see lights descending on cattle and lifting them up, hmmm. The Aztecs and Mayans all did this blood sacrifice type of stuff - like tearing out the heart of human's. The life is in the blood so blood related rituals are very important - it may give these trans-humans, hybrids and grey suits the life that they need to sustain these mutants with human blood.

The blood has this life force essential for the flesh - human life in the first heaven. They may not be able to manifest themselves without this human or animal blood. The Mayans demanded human blood all ancient cultures like these were demonic and occult in nature

These Aliens (you know, these creatures in Grey Suits) are used by Satan as harbingers of perhaps a coming great deception, whereby they for example may appear to deceive the masses (as ambassadors of good will - bearing hi tech gifts and new energy sources, etc.). For now they may be spanning the skies observing what is going on around the world.

These so called "aliens" who are actually Satanic controlled demons occupying "grey suits" continue to experiment with and to mix God's DNA in man. Since Satan cannot create anything all he and his minions can do is mess with God's perfect DNA formula and corrupt the DNA to create a mutated body that they can maintain full control over.

But as already discussed, since the very beginning God forbade this "genetic engineering" (as modern science likes to call it). This is because God knew that this would ultimately create mutants with a propensity for being pure evil, lacking God's Holy Spirit, his blessings, and would be forever lost to Satan with no chance of ever obtaining eternal salvation.

You see nobody, not even supernatural forces can improve on something that was already made perfect in God's eyes; unless that person or entity thinks they are better than God! And of course Satan actually thinks he is! These evil mutations - may perhaps seem superior in certain characteristics to mortal man (just like angels and fallen angels are), but they lack the holy spirit in them, and by virtue of that alone, they are inferior to us.

They are corrupted and thus subject to eternal damnation - not the "immortality" that Satan seduces modern science into endeavoring to achieve. Immortality can only come through the submission and the worship of God the almighty.

Jesus of course had perfect DNA. Adam and Eve also had perfect DNA, until sin (via the forbidden fruit) altered Adam and Eve and consequently our DNA and made us susceptible to all sorts of illnesses and to death. I and others believe that sin can alter our DNA because it opens portals that allow evil to mess with our bodies. However the good news is that when we faithfully obey and follow the Lord our DNA can be once again purified so that we can live a longer, happier and healthier life. But that is a topic for another day!

Sorry for such extreme and bizarre writing here, but the supernatural is just that. It is a realm that we are just not comfortable to write, speak or contemplate. But the supernatural is indeed a realm that exists, and as we get closer to the end of days the supernatural will become more natural, as we witness these events unfolding.

What about the UFO?

I for one and no one that I know have ever witnessed UFO's. That does not mean that others have not witnessed these UFO's. But the real question should be what exactly are these UFOs. Keep in mind that Satan has the power to create these Alien looking creatures and UFO images since he is the prince of the power of the air, and he does control 1/3rd of all angels, the fallen angels also called demons.

These fallen angels can probably take on other forms. Since Satan is the father of lies anything he creates is not real and a counterfeit of what God creates!

In **Revelation 13:13** we learn that Satan can create great signs, even makes fire come down from heaven. So yes, he can surely deceive men with supernatural wonders such as Alien creatures and UFO's. But these are not from superior forms of life from other planets or galaxies! These are just fabrications so that man can believe the extra-terrestrial lies!

UFO sightings seem to be more present during major events such as Israel's formation in 1948, and when Israel re-captured Jerusalem in1967, (are these UFO's actually Satan's version of spy satellites being operated by demons?). Obviously Satan is interested in what happens in Israel which is God's time piece. So are we alone in the Universe? Nope. Satan and his minions occupy the 2nd heaven (the skies).

Chapter 4 - What the Non-Canonical Books Reveal

The books of Jasher, and the book of Enoch (the later regarded as <u>canonical</u> by the <u>Ethiopian Orthodox Tewahedo Church</u> and <u>Eritrean Orthodox Tewahedo Church</u>) tell us all about this. As long as they do not contradict any biblical prophecies or the Canonical writings, then I believe they are

It does appear that the books of **Jubilees and Enoch** are inspired works as they are referenced in the bible, and they support and do not contradict the bible. The book of Jasher is referenced in Joshua 10:13, 2 Samuel 1:18, 2 Timothy 3:8 (it's inferred of here). There are at least 100 references to Enoch in the bible. Even Jesus quoted it, and it was found in the Dead Sea scrolls. This is clearly a book for the end times!

<u>**Jasher 4:18**</u> says "after the angels had revealed the secrets of heaven to mankind, that men then began to teach the blending of one species of animal to another thereby to provoke the Lord" - in **Genesis 1:11,12,21,24,25** we learn that God made animals and all living things (yes even grass, seeds and fruits) to produce only in their own kind and that was what God refers to it being "GOOD". Therefore anything else will only produce evil.

From the beginning everything was to produce according to its own kind. Any mixing or cross-breeding was not good - which means pure EVIL! The only thing that God created that would be in God's image (if it retained in its sinless nature of course) was Man! And so we would have had dominion over all the earth - until we yielded that power to Satan (and we still yield it without the redeeming blood of Lord Jesus).

The Genesis 6 experiment referenced in 9th Jubilee at around 3550 BC (**1 Enoch 6:1,2, and Jubilees 5:1** elaborate even further that Sons of God were fallen angels. Also referred to in **2 Peter 2:4,5, Jude 1:6, Jubilees 5:6**.

Also **Jasher 4:18** and **Jubilees 7:24** confirm that they were mixing animals (the son's of men following after what they were taught by the fallen angels – and everything in their mind was just evil). This is how the Centaurs and other mutations and abominations came to being – the only spirits that can occupy those beasts are the spirits of the Nephilim and demons.
 Perhaps certain species of Dinosaurs came about through this mixing of DNA (Nephilim Animals and beasts).

Dinosaurs may be referenced in Job **40:15-20** where it says that a certain beast "moves its tail like a cedar tree. At least the vegetarian type may be the good kind. But the T-Rex and carnivore class of beasts may have been made by the mixing of DNA? **Genesis 6:12-13 Jubilees 5:2b, and 1 Enoch 7:5**.

God severely judged these fallen angels for mixing the blood (DNA). In **1 Enoch 10:9-12** we learn that God limited the 1st generation Nephilim to 500 years (and they would kill themselves off while the "watchers" watched them kill themselves off! – And God asked Michael to bind Semjaza the head Archon for 70 generations 70 x 70.

The judgment against the watchers was extremely severe; their height dropped much from (300 Cubits – same length as Noah's Ark) 450 feet down to 35 feet. **Genesis 6:12** the whole earth became corrupted 5 times over - so God had to destroy it all and start over.

1 Enoch 6:2-4 – the fallen angels feared the punishment for this great sin but they all made an oath to sin as a whole group – as if that would exonerate them! They asked Enoch to intercede for their sin -**1 Enoch 13:3-5**

1 Enoch 68:5 – they alone will ever be judged for this act again – that is how great the judgment would be.

Jubilees 5:12 – explains the judgment of the fallen angels. "And God made it so they could never breed again". Daniel 2:43 or 3:43 also prophesied that it would never happen again.

Chapter 5 - Supernatural Forces and the End of Days

There is no doubt that these evil supernatural forces are engaged in a cosmic battle with God's angelic beings, and

they are fighting fiercely for eternal control of our souls. This cosmic battle will ultimately lead to the end of days.

Mathew 24:37 teaches us that the last days will be just Like in the days of Noah. So just like the days of Noah which resulted

in the great flood, the last days will result in another worldwide calamity - but this time it won't be due to a flood.

Just like before the great flood of Noah's time, we find ourselves still engaging in genetic engineering to modify DNA for supposedly the "better good" of mankind. Today, Institutions, Universities and Corporations throughout the world engage in all types of genetic alterations.

They experiment on animals, plants, seeds, humans and just about anything that they can lay their hands on. Are any of these modified foods or seeds better for us? I guess it depends on what you mean by "better" - better for who? In any event time will tell just how safe all of these genetically enhanced and altered organisms will be for our bodies. Unable or unwilling to heed God's warnings, man once again is provoking God to put an end to all civilization.

Like the Nazi's before them, certain modern day "institutions" secretly want to reverse engineer the gods (the Nephilim) back into existence. Not to side track but the word holocaust means burnt Offering; but these burnt offerings intentionally or unintentionally opened up evil portals for our modern times. The Holocaust opened portals that allowed the Lucifer movement by Satan to strengthen – it was like 6 million blood offerings upon the alter of Satan!

Noah lived 950 years – 600 years before and 350 years after the flood (**Genesis 6:12**). It was during the time of Noah that people started to play God and mix species (mix DNA). It appears that before the great flood, the fallen angels had revealed allot of advanced knowledge and secrets, but unfortunately this was to be used for their evil intentions!

Note: Modern science (due to ignorance of the word of God) likes to refer to these knowledgeable beings as "ancient astronauts or aliens" instead of demons or fallen angels.

After the flood this advanced knowledge was suppressed (probably by God and for our own good) for thousands of years. Over the last 100 years or so however, there has been an explosion of knowledge. Today, computing power increases exponentially every year.

Enoch 10:12 teaches us that the fallen angels would be locked up for 70 generations 70 years x 70 generations comes to 4,900 years. Take 4900 years from 3000 BC (Noah's time and the times when the Nephilim occupied the earth) brings us to the beginning of 1900. Although technological advances can be good and convenient, remember that this knowledge can come from evil in order to enable man to develop technologies that can also destroy all of mankind (like they tried to do already as we learned in Genesis 6 and as discussed above)! **1 Enoch 8:1** may reveal that Azazel (a fallen angel) taught men how to build bombs!

From 1900 we went from horse and buggy to planes, and rocket propelled probes past Pluto, the Hubel telescope, Nuclear Bombs, unimagined computing power, and many more technological advances. More than 2053 nuclear bombs have gone off from 1945 to 1998! As was prophesied in **Daniel 12:4** "many shall run to and fro and Knowledge shall increase" during the time of the end!   How can anyone doubt, if just with this prophecy alone, that we are indeed living in the end times.

Will all this knowledge lead to much good for mankind in the coming years. Of course not! It will be used for much evil - to the point that Jesus will have to return to prevent a total annihilation of mankind **Mathew 24:22**. The knowledge could also be referring to the knowledge of evil (genetic engineering, Genome, and altering of DNA).

Science is rushing to achieve what is termed as the "Singularity"; this is where machines become smarter and more intellectual than humans. This is also termed as Artificial Intelligence, or artillects. This of course is another satanic plot to replace man with part human part machine mutations, and of course to try to reduce humans as mutations void of God's spirit, and to have us think that we are an inferior race and that Satan has the power to improve on God's creation.

This is a plot to replace God's perfectly created human beings with a demonic and evil counterfeit. A recent Time magazine article said that **by 2045 man becomes immortal as we become "manchines;** part man yet part machine.

Trans humanism is the idea that we can permanently alter the human race with artificial intelligence systems so that we can be supernatural; to create a superior model of humans with robotics, etc. like what Hitler wanted.

In **nickbostrom.com** – it talks about how we are going to merge with animals to get superior hearing, sight, including seeing into the spirit realm/supernatural dimensions - the never ending quest to communicate with the supernatural.

Today's laptop stores more information than the Cray computers of the 1950's! This technological explosion is great as long as the world uses it for good, and let's hope we use it better than with the development of Nuclear fusion - the later being an explosion that none of us want to experience!

But here again the news is somber as the bible reveals that in the last days there will be calamities that seem to mimic the effects of a nuclear holocaust. They could of course be referring to some other cause (like a large comet or meteor striking the earth), but the outcome nevertheless is the same.

The following bible verses are just a few that describe what appears to be nuclear explosions and the side effect thereof:
Revelation 6:12-14
Revelation 8:7-10
Revelation 16:3-4
Revelation 18:8-10;
Revelation 18:17-19

We will discuss these supernatural forces a bit more in the next chapter.

Chapter 6 - The Book of Revelation and Supernatural forces

We learn in **Revelation 9:11** (easy to remember: 911!) that the beast that comes out of the bottomless pit is what the Greeks referred to as Apollo. Apollo which is referred to as Apollyon here - is another name for Nimrod.

Joel 2:3-8 as well as Revelation 9:7-10 – may be alluding to the return of the Nephilim in the last days. By the way, the 200 million army (**Revelation 9:16**) may not necessarily be the Chinese and Asian armies as many have believed in the past and may actually be the Locusts from the bottomless pit referred to in Rev 9:3.

Keep in mind that there are only about 70 million horses in the world today, so that 200,000,000 men on horses must be referring to some other beast being described by John (as best as he can given the incredible visions that he is taking in). Isaiah 13:21-22, and Rev 9 hint that these **200 million men on horses could in actuality be Centaurs strait from the pit. After all,** Apollo (Rev 9:11) is the originator of Centaurus – the Centaurs, Joel 2, Math 24:37, all hint that Nephilim will return.

Since Satan knows that the life is in the blood (**Leviticus 17:11**) and all occult practices and rituals are blood focused, I believe that the mark of the beast may involve our blood and the altering of our DNA (just like in the times of Noah) in some form or another.

The mark may be comprised of an injection with the DNA of say Apollo (Satan's blood!!!). Thus Satan would corrupt our DNA making whoever takes his mark to be forever his and it would therefore be impossible for this person to ever be able to enter God's kingdom.

This may be why those who take the mark of the beast as so harshly - read **Revelation 14:9-10**!!! That would also be why Revelation makes this condemnation so final, and why we would never be able to be redeemable back to God (for it is an unpardonable sin!).

Chapter 7 - Conclusion

The book of Revelation is full of prophecy that seems more like science fiction than reality. Well given all that we have explored in this book I hope you can see that all of these "symbolic"

creatures and beasts referenced in bible prophecy may indeed be the reality during the last 7 years of this age (referred to as the tribulation period).

All of these God replacing occult practices that are as old as adultery continue today unabated. In our time the genetic breeding of Nephilim with animal and human DNA in laboratories is an attempt to create a new race of god-men or supermen. This science is called Trans-humanism and it is an attempt to scientifically evolve the human race into gods. **Just like us mortal men, we think we know more than our creator GOD!**

How could God allow all of this evil, you may be thinking. God has clearly bound himself so that everything that goes on in this planet - man will be free to execute (Good or bad). See 2 Timothy 1:7, John 16:33, 1 John 4:4. God wants us to see how clearly hopeless man is without God in this life and world.

Satan wants us to think that we are just animals like the monkey or a rat, by influencing the fabrication of such false belief systems as the theory of evolution. He wants us to think that we are hopeless sinners unworthy of becoming children of God (since he cannot). He wants us to think he does not exist, yet in the background Satan is working 24 – 7 to keep us from attaining eternal life with God and Jesus, since Satan hates all that is God and good!

Yet how much clearer can God have been when he declares in **Genesis 1:26 that he created man in his image and likeness!**

Satan hates God because Satan hates the light and the truth – he is the father of lies. He hates that God has replaced him and will eventually put him away. He hates man, because he knows that God plans to eventually reproduce himself through Mankind (his God family). We through the holy spirit and by the redemptive blood of the lamb of God that takes away the sins of the world – Jesus Christ; will become children of the most high! And Satan hates this!

Technological advances can be used for good, and in some cases are. But here we are, in these last days and our world is totally distracted by all the pleasures of the many technological gadgets and toys of these modern times.

We are distracted by all of this social media gossip, rather than using these modern day tools to share the good news of the Kingdom of God to this fallen world. We would rather share pictures, jokes and anything, as long as it has nothing to do with the God of the bible. Yet all around us we are hemorrhaging and experiencing the convulsive birth pains that Jesus Christ outlined in the signs of the times foretold in **Mathew chapter 24**.

One way Satan will attack us is by keeping us busy and distracted with the endless preoccupations of life. This way we have no time for God. He makes us lazy for the word. Satan will provide many of us with many excuses for avoiding prayer and time in the Word. He will tempt us with worldly things.

How to protect ourselves from the deceptions of Satan and his Fallen Angels: Put on the Full Armor of God:

"**Put on the whole armor of God that** ye may be able to stand against the wiles of the devil. For we wrestle not against flesh and blood, but against principalities, against powers, against the rulers of the darkness of this world, against spiritual wickedness in high places." **(Ephesians 6:11-12)**

In America, I read somewhere that the fastest growing religion is "witchcraft" (yes they even call that a religion!). People in these last days are oblivious to just how dangerous and serious it is to embrace the occult.

When we make light of God and his word, we open the doors to a supernatural realm that (without God) you are not equipped to fight on your own.

Instead of embracing and becoming experts in the occult, and the paranormal, we should strive to become experts in the word of God. There are plenty of supernatural teachings throughout the bible.

**So instead of wanting to learn about man's version of the supernatural, why not learn the supernatural as taught by the creator of all things both natural and supernatural, seen and unseen.** So let's close by committing to Ephesians 6:11-12, by putting on the whole armor of God against Satan and his deceptive evil and lies.

Society seems to embrace a "perfect" society that is void of God and his laws. Hmmm, just like the "utopic" one world Government, and religious system that Satan is planning for all mankind!

In the mean time I have no doubt that all the leading Nations are tripping over each other racing to get ahead of this "human enhancement technology" revolution - in order to win the next wars! Of course this is Satan's plan and of course this plan will also fail.

God will not allow it, because God is in full control, despite what fallen man thinks. God just lets Satan and fallen man dig their own graves along with his fallen angels, demons, nephilim and alien creatures.

I hope you have enjoyed this book as I have enjoyed writing it. The supernatural realm is fascinating. It can be very unsettling for those who have not accepted Jesus Christ as Lord and savior.

Only Christ is worthy and able to conquer Satan and herald in the only "new world order" that will matter in the end - the Kingdom of God! There is only ONE way to peace and "order" in this world, and it is through the prince of peace.

Despite all of the craziness we endure in these last days, Revelation 19 and 20 gives us great reassurance that despite all of Satan's evil plans to undermine God's plan for mankind...*in the end we win!*

After all, the good side always wins in...
the end!

Bonus Chapter:

This complimentary chapter is an excerpt (chapter 7) from my brand new book published on 1/1/2015:
"*Apocalypse Countdown - 2015 to 2021*"

Chapter 7 - The Book of Revelation and the Apocalypse

While the prior chapter was date specific relative to heavenly signs and appointed feast days that could be harbingers of the apocalypse. We will now discover the events and the series of judgments that will unfold once the apocalypse begins.

The book of Revelation is appropriately the last book of the bible, because it is primarily the **go to book on the last days of this age**. It also is the revelation of Jesus Christ in that it reveals that Jesus Christ was and is the Messiah, and He will return to rule the world at the conclusion of this age of man. God allowed man 6,000 years to mess everything up and prove that **without the Spirit of God** mankind has always and will always be unable to resist the temptations of their carnal spirit which makes them susceptible to the cunning of Satan and his dark evil influences, which has and will ultimately lead this world to its demise.

To stay in topic let's review the key clues in the book of Revelation regarding the apocalypse and what types of events are revealed to take place before during and after the great tribulation period (apocalypse).

The apostle John was in exile in the Island of Patmos by the Romans because of his testimony of Jesus. While in exile, he received many visions from Jesus and some of His angels. John could only describe these visions symbolically as they were for the last days; the days that you and I live in. So the description of these visions can be quite confusing to the untrained mind. Since my book is about the time of the end I will only cover the key prophecies of Revelation pertaining to our time.

Before we begin, keep in mind that in many end time prophecies duality comes into play, representing visions and prophecies that may apply to more than one nation, time in history, and meaning. For example when one reads of Babylon, it may refer to ancient Babylon or to Babylon of the last days. With careful study and cross referencing of scriptures, you can and will correctly interpret the prophecies. With that said let's move on to the phases of judgments during the apocalypse.

Rev. Chapter 6 and 7 - Jesus has a scroll in his hand with 7 seals. When He opens the seals of the scroll - each one announces the Judgments that are to come upon the whole earth. The first four scrolls reveal the four horsemen of the apocalypse. These are not literal men riding on horses but rather they are symbolic of the events that will be unfolding during the great tribulation (apocalypse). I believe these events will occur in rapid succession one after another; hence the vision of horses in motion; one immediately after the other.

The Seven Seal Judgments

The 1st Seal is the first horse - a white horse whose rider has a bow but no arrows. This may be describing **the Antichrist** (man of perdition) that is to come, masquerading as a savior with peaceful intentions, and thus conquering an unsuspecting world through deceptive means (**Rev. 6:2**).

The 2nd Seal is the second horse - a rider on a red horse carrying a great sword to take peace from the earth, **so that people could kill one another**. This is clearly symbolizing war among the nation - perhaps **World War III** (**Rev. 6:4**).

The 3rd Seal is the third horse - a rider on a black horse carrying scales on his hand and based on what is said in this passage, it is revealing **a great famine throughout the world**; a great shortage of food supplies as a result of devastated lands due to the war released by the second seal (**Rev. 5-6**)

The 4th Seal is the fourth horse - a rider on an ashen (grayish green) horse symbolizing death and hell. This rider is **symbolic of the beast kingdom consisting of the ten nation confederacy**. Notice that the rider is referring to "*them*" and not "*him*". It further states that "power was given to them over a fourth of the earth, to kill with sword, with hunger, with death, and the beasts of the earth." I believe this fourth rider is the final beast kingdom under control of the man of perdition that destroys 1/4th of the earth - possibly with weapons of mass destruction! I believe that the "**beasts of the earth**" is NOT referring to lions, bears and other predator animals but rather the leaders of the beast kingdom, consisting of the ten nation confederacy and the henchmen that martyr the saints as we read in the fifth seal that follows.

Note: The term "*beast*" refers to the beast kingdom and all the people that associate with it, and who worship the beast (Satan) and take his mark (the mark of the beast).

5th Seal - reveals a great persecution and Martyrdom of a myriad of saints by the beast kingdom because of their testimony/witness of the name of Jesus Christ as the son of God in accordance with the word of God, in the Holy bible. These who are referred to as "**saints**" are the Christians and elect who are beheaded or killed by other means because they do not bow down and worship the Antichrist (Satan's man of perdition), who has come to full power over the earth after the fourth seal above.

Important Note: The revelation clearly reveals that the saints (all Christians - the body of Christ) will be targeted and hated not just by the one world government but most of the inhabitants of the world who will be brainwashed into believing that the antichrist is God, and the false prophet is Jesus! That is why they will gladly take the mark of the beast. This hatred towards all witnesses of the Lord is clearly revealed in various places including **Rev. 11:10**, when the inhabitants of the earth celebrate when the two witnesses appointed by God to witness to the world in an effort to save as many souls as possible, are killed by the man of perdition (Satan's representative on earth).

6th Seal - A great Earthquake rocks the planet.

7th Seal - when the seventh seal is released, there is silence in Heaven for 1/2 hour, and seven angels are given seven trumpets in preparation of the release of the trumpet judgments of God. This appears to be a transition point, a short period of rest, perhaps to allow for some to repent before the trumpet judgments begin.

NOTE: This period of rest at the seventh seal is interesting when we consider that the Lord rested on the seventh day and sanctified it (made it Holy), and

how he commands you and I to do the same. Obviously
the Sabbath day was never abolished as it is
symbolically observed even in heaven during the
apocalypse, and it is one of the Ten Commandments
(**Exodus 20:8-11**). This may be another main reason
why the **seventh seal** does not release any judgments
upon the earth! When you study Revelation carefully as
I have, you will perceive the level of perfect precision on
how even the last seven years of the age of man unfold.
It is like a religious or holy ceremony in heaven
commemorating the end of this imperfect age.

The first 6 seals of Revelation chapter six appear to be a
synopsis of the key events that will occur during the
great tribulation, which *will **NOT** begin* until the man of
perdition is finally revealed.

Note that these seal judgments are not necessarily
direct judgments from God, but rather judgments and
curses that man has brought upon himself by placing
their faith in man, instead of in God!

The Seven Trumpet Judgments

**Now let's move on to the seven trumpet
judgments**:

The trumpet Judgments are sounded by seven Angels. These angels are charged with executing God's judgments; the "wrath of God judgments". We can infer from **Rev. 6:10-11** that these judgments come upon the earth in large part because of the blood of the saints (God's children, the body of Christ) that was shed because of their testimony of God's word:

1) The first angel sounded his trumpet - **which destroys all green grass, and _a third_ of all trees**. (**Rev. 8:7**). This would obviously lead to a global famine, and many millions would die of starvation.

So the **first trumpet** appears to be describing a thermonuclear attack that destroys a third of earth (Note that the western hemisphere is one third of the earth). **A third of the trees** were burned up as well as all green grass. One can imagine the enormous loss of life and the magnitude of the pestilence and famine that would affect the entire earth when one third of all trees are vaporized and **_all green grass_** (i.e. vegetation) is burned up.

2) The second angel sounds his trumpet and a great mountain falls on the sea and a third of the sea became blood. This is NOT a literal mountain or literal blood, but is John's way of describing perhaps **a large asteroid** or **nuclear missiles** that land in the ocean and contaminate one third of the ocean water. As a direct result, **_one third_** of all sea creatures perish, and one third of the ships at sea are destroyed. Most likely tsunamis will also wreak havoc on many coastal areas (**Rev. 8:8-9**).

3) When the third angel sounds his trumpet - a great star fell from heaven burning like a torch, and this one contaminates **one third** of the rivers and springs of water, many men perish from drinking this water. This one may be caused by nuclear weapons (or again asteroids), because the description "burning like a torch" is more descriptive of an intercontinental ballistic missile (ICBM), and it contaminates drinking water, causing many people die from drinking it. Perhaps they are not aware of the level of radiation in this water thinking that the contamination is not so widespread (**Rev. 8:10-11**).

So this star is most likely one or several nuclear missiles impacting a land mass with rivers and springs of water. We also read here that a third of the earth is darkened due to this nuclear attack on an area of the globe, resulting in great death.

4) The fourth angel sounded and "*a third* of the sun, moon, and stars were struck, so that a third of them were darkened and a third of the day did not shine (**Rev. 8:12**). This must mean that one third of the earth has been devastated either by a massive asteroid impact or thermo-nuclear exchange or related catastrophe.

Make note that so far **_one third_** of the earth's land mass is affected by the first four trumpet blasts? God is placing great emphasis on this, which leads me to believe that the great tribulation will begin when a large land and ocean area of the world is devastated.

In **Rev. 8:13** we are warned that the next 3 trumpet judgments are going to make things even worse for the remaining inhabitants of the earth.

Note: Given the **Rev. 8:13** warning, it is hard to imagine as I write this in early December 2014, how progressively bad things will actually get. This is **_probably because at this point the restrainer is removed_** from the earth giving Satan power to wreak maximum havoc over this planet.
We should all **_pray_** that God indeed will rapture His elect - the church (the body of Christ) before the great tribulation begins, as many theologians believe (Pre-tribulation rapture)! But when we read in the revelations that a myriad (millions) of saints will be martyred during the apocalypse, one must wonder and prepare for a mid or post rapture of the saints. Regardless, we must remain prepared and ready since our appointed time to meet our maker can be at any moment.

5) The fifth angel sounds his trumpet - A Star (perhaps a fallen angel) falls from heaven and has been given the key to the bottomless pit (Hades/hell). He opens the bottomless pit and smoke arose out of the pit like the smoke of a great furnace (**Rev. 9:1-2**). This may be describing a massive volcanic eruption which also shoots out smoke just like a great furnace!

The fifth trumpet also releases evil spirits from Hades who afflict all men except the 144,000 who have the seal of God on their forehead and who have been granted special protection from God (**Rev. 9:3-11**).

The locusts that arise out of the bottomless pit as a result of the fifth trumpet could be some form of **germ warfare** or **manufactured virus** since they do not harm the vegetation but only the inhabitants of the earth; specifically those who do not have the seal of God on their forehead (i.e. the 144,000). This germ or virus apparently affects the body for five months; perhaps a vaccine is developed to curtail the pandemic. Jesus does warn in **Mathew 24**, that the end of day judgments will include pestilence and disease (such as the Ebola virus outbreak of 2014).

Note: The revelation that demons are instructed to afflict only the non-believers, should be a reminder to all that Satan is NOT even a friend to the non-believers. Satan does not discriminate, he hates anything associated with God and equally, and is bent on destroying it all and taking it all to hell with him. This includes the grass, trees, planet earth and all human beings which were all created in the image of God.

6) The sixth angel sounds his trumpet - and four *fallen* Angels which were bound at the Euphrates River are released (**Rev. 9:14-15**). These evil angelic beings were so powerful that they had to be physically restrained until this moment in time.

The Euphrates River runs through Iraq. This may be indicating that the area of Iraq (where the terror army called ISIS is presently based), and the Middle East as a whole may be ground zero for the establishment of the beast kingdom and headquarters of the man of perdition. Also interesting how this area of the Middle East has always been an area of Jewish and Christian intolerance and persecution.

These four fallen angels kill a third of mankind, with a massive 200,000,000 man army which once the demonic influences are released in that region, invade from the east.

They are able to do this by influencing an army of 200 million; this may be a continuation or beginning of World War III that was announced at the opening of the aforementioned second and fourth seals.

Note: In John's time an army that size was impossible. Today it is quite possible considering the nearly seven billion worldwide population. We also discover that this army will kill one third of mankind with the use of weapons that rain down fire and brimstone **which again reads to me like nuclear weaponry** (**Rev. 9:15-18**).

Rev. 9:20-21 makes it clear why these judgments continue to persist to the very end, as those who survive through all of the prior judgments still refuse to repent from worshipping demons, idols, sorcery, murder, sexual immorality and thefts.

The seventh angel sounds his trumpet and we have another break from the Judgments; ***another Sabbath break*** in between the trumpet and the final bowl judgments. Victory is proclaimed in heaven and a celebration commences as the angels and elders announce that the kingdoms of this world are now the kingdoms of the Lord; as the Messiah prepares for His triumphant second coming!

The Sabbath is to be a day where we stop all work and worship the Lord; thanking Him for the prior week's blessings. On this day we pray, nourish our spirit with the word, and develop our relationship with the Lord. We saw that after the sixth seal was released, Revelation chapter seven is an instructional chapter.

Once again after the sixth trumpet judgment in Revelation chapter nine, chapter ten is also an instructional chapter right through Rev. 11 verse 14 when the seventh trumpet judgment is released.

After the seventh trumpet judgment, Revelation chapters 12 through 15 are instructional chapters as well which describe the following:

Rev. Ch. 12: This chapter covers the cosmic battle that Satan has waged against Israel, and mankind. Note that he is NO MATCH to Jesus and God, so that he can only attempt to defeat Jesus and God through mankind! ***Satan knows he already lost his battle against the Messiah almost 2,000 years ago when Jesus Christ became our sacrificial Lamb at the cross, allowing anyone who acknowledges and accepts His sacrifice the right to become children of the Most High***! Messiah has *already* earned the deed to planet earth and the universe. In His mercy He is just waiting for the full number of saved souls to be reached before He returns (**Rev. 6:10-11**)!

Rev. Ch. 13: This chapter describes the antichrist, false prophet and the beast kingdom that will reign approximately three and one half years before the second coming.

Rev. Ch. 14 and 15: are celebratory chapters in heaven whereby the angels and the saints (all those who were previously martyred because they refused the mark of Satan) prepare for the final series of judgments and the return of the Messiah to establish a new heaven and a new earth - one that is purified, and cleansed of all sin). Some scholars believe that by this point the rapture may have already occurred.

The Final Seven Bowl Judgments

Now we move on to the last series of judgments; the Bowl (also referred to as vial) judgments. Like the Trumpet judgments, the bowl judgments are also a part of the "**Wrath of God Judgments**". This series of judgments appears to be particularly for those who accepted the mark of Satan (mark of the beast), and all who refuse to repent.

1) The first Bowl is poured out and a horrible sore *afflicts all those who took the mark of the beast (Satan) and who worshiped his image*.
I hope that you like I are finding it really hard to comprehend how so many will be so deceived by Satan in these last days into thinking that this coming demon possessed one world government leader of the final one world government is God or can actually defeat and or prevent the second coming of Messiah.

2) The second bowl is poured out on the sea and it became blood (contaminated). This time all the living creatures of the sea are dead (not just one third).

3) The third bowl is poured on all rivers and springs of water so that no drinkable water remains.

4) The fourth bowl is poured out and the sun scorches men with fire. Perhaps the ozone layer fails amidst all the level of contamination and radiation in the atmosphere.

5) The fifth bowl immerses the beast kingdom (the one world empire) in total darkness. I perceive that since with the fourth bowl there is a sun that scorches men with fire the sun now fries out the electrical grid (**Rev. 16:10-11**)

6) The sixth bowl dries up the Euphrates River which allows an army from the east (king of the East) the ability to cross over to engage in the **battle of Armageddon** along with other invading armies. This last battle is referred to as "**the great day of God Almighty**" (**Rev. 16:14**), probably because it brings an end to the age of man.

On or around the battle of Armageddon the Lord returns as we read in the verse that follows:

Rev. 16:15

"Behold, I am coming as a thief. Blessed is he who watches, and keeps his garments, lest he walks naked and they see his shame."

7 the seventh bowl judgment: After the seventh bowl judgment is poured out on the air a great voice declares ***"it is done"*** which releases the greatest earthquake in history. It must break the Richter scale along with everything else since the force of this quake collapses mountains and Islands.

This massive earthquake is the final event of the age of man as the remaining chapters of Revelation are instructional as follows:

Revelation 17 & 18: These are two very important prophecy chapters that describe who or what "**Babylon the Great**" is. This great entity is so important to end time events that God dedicates two full chapters to this topic. This will be covered in detail in another chapter.

Rev. 19: Describes the Messiah's second coming, with Jesus returning with His heavenly army to put an end to Satan and his minions. It also describes the Marriage Supper of the Lamb.

Rev. 20: Describes the Judgment of the antichrist, false prophet, Satan, the demons, zombies (sorry, I couldn't help it!), and all those who took the mark of the beast.

Rev. Chapter 21 - Describes the new Heavens and new earth - our glorious new home through eternity!

In Chapter 22: The revelation of Jesus Christ culminates in His words:

"I, Jesus, have sent my angel to give you this testimony for the churches. I am the Root and the Offspring of David, and the bright Morning Star."

My brothers and sisters in the Lord, as you now know, many prophetic signs are converging in 2015, making it quite possible that 2015 may be the harbinger year, warning that the apocalypse is imminent. So I believe that this book is one of the most important publications that I have ever penned.

Among the many crucial end time prophecies and topics that you will discover in Apocalypse Countdown - 2015 - 2021 are:

- Discover all of the key prophecies from all of the great ancient prophets; the key signs of the time of the end
- 2015 - the Harbinger Year
- Where is America in Bible Prophecy?
- The rise of America
- The coming fall of America
- Who is Babylon the Great - America?
- Why will Babylon the Great be Destroyed?
- Who will Destroy Babylon the great?
- How will Babylon the Great be Destroyed?
- Where will the antichrist establish his headquarters
- What nations will comprise the ten nation end time Empire
- Why is Jerusalem such a Burdensome Stone?
- What are the Consequences of Dividing up God's Land?
- The mystery of the Shemita blessings and curses.
- The Jubilee year connection
- The month of September and its link to financial and national disasters.
- Why there is more to 9/11 than most think?
- The coming seven trumpet judgments
- Who is the Beast of Revelation?
- Who is the 666 - the antichrist?
- Why will so many take the Mark of the Beast?
- The antichrist will come out of which Nation?
- Who are the Kings of North and South?
- Where is "Satan's throne" located?
- Left behind? What the prophecies reveal about the Rapture
- How to Survive the Coming Apocalypse
- Apocalypse Survival supplies and tips
- Emergency Supplies

- How to Prepare Emotionally and Mentally
- And more!

Again, I am not saying that 2015 is the year, but rather that from 2015 to 2021 we may indeed experience such great unrest and calamities throughout the world as discussed in this book, so that the controlling majority who are **void of the spirit of the living God** will force an unholy union in hopes for security. Tragically the security they secure will be a false security strait from hell!

This was a complimentary chapter from my new release:
"Apocalypse Countdown - 2015 to 2021"

Get Complimentary Access to: "Prophecy Alerts"

Dear Reader: Prophecies are being fulfilled so rapidly in these last days that I am offering my readers complimentary access to "*prophecy alerts*" so that you get "*Breaking Prophecy News*" as soon as it breaks...Just follow this link below and sign Up today...

http://robertritebooks.com/prophecy-alerts/

I appreciate your review of this book

If you liked this eBook, you may want to consider the following related publications...

Related Books by Robert Rite....

- "Apocalypse Timeline - 2015 to 2021"

- "Revelation Mysteries Decoded: Unlocking the Secrets of the coming Apocalypse"

- "Signs in the Heavens, Divine Secrets of the Zodiac & the Blood Moons of 2014!"

- "Apocalypse Codes - Decoding the Prophecies in the Book of Daniel"

- "Ancient Apocalypse Codes"

- "Aliens, Fallen Angels, Nephilim and the Supernatural"

- "Be healed!....How to Unlock the Supernatural Healing Power of God"

- "Awaken the Supernatural You!"

- "Blood Moons Rising"

- "Bible Verses for Supernatural Blessings"

- "128 Powerful Bible Verses that can Save Your Life!"

Available at Amazon and other distribution channels.

I appreciate your positive feedback

1) Visit and like our page at
https://www.facebook.com/RobertRiteBooks

2) Tweet "I recommend reading books @Robert Rite

3) Write a review on amazon.com or goodreads.com

4) Enjoy many articles at my blog: http://bible-blog.org

CPSIA information can be obtained
at www.ICGtesting.com
Printed in the USA
LVHW082100040520
654960LV00024B/3527

9 781493 775750